Start TO Finish
Second Series

FROM Bulb TO Tulip

LISA OWINGS

LERNER PUBLICATIONS Minneapolis

TABLE OF Contents

Lerner Publications Company
A division of Lerner Publishing Group, Inc.
241 First Avenue North
Minneapolis, MN 55401 USA

For reading levels and more information, look up this title at www.lernerbooks.com.

Library of Congress Cataloging-in-Publication Data

Owings, Lisa.
    From bulb to tulip / by Lisa Owings.
        pages   cm. — (Start to finish. Second series)
    Includes index.
    ISBN 978-1-4677-6021-8 (lib. bdg. : alk. paper)
    ISBN 978-1-4677-6285-4 (EB pdf)
    1. Tulips—Juvenile literature. I. Title. II. Series: Start to finish (Minneapolis, Minn.). Second series.
SB413.T9O95 2015
635.9'3432—dc23   2014018980

Manufactured in the United States of America
2 – HF – 1/15/16

Tulips are so beautiful. How do they grow?

First, gardeners buy tulip bulbs.

Tulips grow from bulbs. Gardeners can choose from a variety of tulip bulbs. The different bulbs **bloom** into a rainbow of colors, from bright reds and yellows to soft pinks and deep purples. Some tulips have many colors.

They plant the bulbs in the fall.

Gardeners plant tulip bulbs in the fall. First, they dig holes 6 to 10 inches (15 to 25 centimeters) deep. Then they plant the bulbs with the round ends down and the pointy ends up. They cover the bulbs with soil.

Next, they water the bulbs.

After planting, gardeners water the bulbs. This gives the tulip plants a head start in putting down **roots** before the ground freezes.

Then gardeners wait for spring.

The tulip bulbs continue to slowly grow their roots during winter. Tulips need this period of cold weather to bloom. In warm **climates**, tulip bulbs are chilled for several weeks before planting.

In spring, the tulips sprout.

The tulip bulbs sprout when the weather gets warm enough in the spring. Green leaves **emerge** from the pointy tips of the bulbs. They slowly push up through the soil.

Then the tulips grow.

Each day, the tulip plants grow a little taller. The first leaves fall away from the stem as new leaves grow up between them. The youngest leaves unfold to reveal a green tulip bud.

Finally, the tulips bloom!

The tulip buds open, and the flowers show off their bright colors. During the day, the blooms spread their petals wide. At night, the flowers close their petals tightly.

After blooming, the tulips store energy.

Soon the blooms begin to fade. Gardeners remove the **withering** blooms. The leaves continue to gather energy from the sun. The tulip plants store this energy in their bulbs for the next year.

The next year, they bloom again!

With proper care, tulips can bloom for years. Try planting some this fall. Then enjoy their beauty for many springs to come!

Glossary

bloom: to produce flowers. The flowers are also called blooms.

bulbs: onion-shaped parts of some plants that stay underground and grow into new plants

climates: the typical weather patterns of certain areas

emerge: to come out from a hidden place

energy: usable power that allows plants to grow

roots: parts of plants that grow underground, collecting water and nutrients and holding the plant in place

withering: drying up and becoming weak

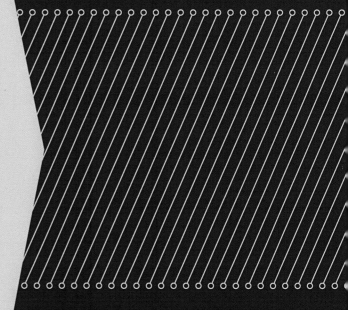

Further Information

Behind the Scenes: Tulip Time-Lapse Video
http://www.buschgardensvablog.com/behind-scenes-tulip-time-lapse-video
Watch a time-lapse video of a tulip growing, and read about how the video was made.

Noyes, Deborah. *Hana in the Time of the Tulips.* Cambridge, MA: Candlewick, 2004. Follow Hana's story as she grows up in Holland during a time period known as tulip mania.

Rajczak, Kristen. *Watch Tulips Grow.* New York: Gareth Stevens, 2011. Read this book to learn more about the tulip's life cycle.

Sterling, Kristin. *Exploring Flowers.* Minneapolis: Lerner Publications, 2012. Explore all kinds of flowers and what they have in common in this book.

Tulip Facts for Kids
http://www.sciencekids.co.nz/sciencefacts/plants/tulips.html
Check out this website to learn lots of cool facts about tulips.

Index

Photo Acknowledgments

The images in this book are used with the permission of:
© Melpomenem/iStock/Thinkstock, p. 1; © alexlukin/
iStock/Thinkstock, p. 3; © iStockphoto.com/whitemay, p. 5;
© Liane Matrisch/Hemera/Thinkstock, p. 7; © Courtesy
Netherland Bulb Company, p. 9; © vlad_karavaev/iStock/
Thinkstock, p. 11; © Adrian C. Nitu/Alamy, p. 13; © Robert
Byron/Hemera/Thinkstock, p. 15; © Fuse/Thinkstock,
p. 17; © Catherine Paffey/Alamy, p. 19; © goce/iStock/
Thinkstock, p. 21.

Front cover: © dreamaway/Shutterstock.com.

Main body text set in Arta Std Book 20/26.
Typeface provided by International Typeface Corp.